Groveton High School Library
38 State St.
Groveton, NH 03582

D0891802

Journey to the Outer Planets

Today's World in Space

Journey to the Outer Planets

By David Baker

Rourke Enterprises, Inc.
Vero Beach, FL 32964

© 1988 Rourke Enterprises, Inc.

All rights reserved. No part of this book may be reproduced or utilized in any form or by any means, electronic or mechanical including photocopying, recording or by any information storage and retrieval system without permission in writing from the publisher.

Library of Congress Cataloging-in-Publication Data

Baker, David, 1944-
   Journey to the outer planets. / David L. Baker

   p. cm. — (Today's world in space)
   Bibliography: p.
   Includes index.
   Summary: Discusses humanity's exploration of the planets in our solar system,with an emphasis on the unmanned space flights to the gas giants on the outside of the system.
   1. Planets—Exploration—Juvenile literature.
[1. Planets—Exploration.] I. Title. II. Series: Baker, David, 1944-   . Today's world in space.
QB602.B35 1987   919.9'2'04-dc19   87-19888
ISBN 0-86592-405-8   CIP
                                                            AC

CONTENTS

The Solar System

Earth and its neighbor worlds are part of a great family of objects orbiting the sun. This family contains not only planets and their moons but *asteroids, meteorites, comets,* and millions of rocky fragments left over from the birth of the solar system billions of years ago. The *solar system* is the collection of everything in *orbit* around the sun and may extend many times beyond the outermost planet, Pluto.

The best way to consider the solar system is to look first at the sun's history. All the other objects in the solar system are there because of the sun — or, rather, because of what happened when the sun was formed. That story began around 5,000 million years ago when the sun took shape from a cloud of gases whirling

Our solar system consists of the sun, nine planets, asteroids, and comets. It belongs to a galaxy similar to Andromeda seen here.

around in the *galaxy.*

The galaxy is a collection of more than 100 million stars, clouds of dust, gas, and rocky fragments. Galaxies are probably as old as the universe itself, which scientists now estimate to be from 10,000 to 12,000 million years old. Stars are huge balls of compressed gas within which nuclear reactions are taking place continuously. *Atoms* of *hydrogen* are fused together to form heavier elements. They give off energy in the form of radiation and light.

The sun was formed when pressures from nearby exploding stars squeezed gases together. As the size of the compressed ball of gases got bigger, *gravity* took over and sucked everything into the middle. When that happened the whole sphere, called a *nebula,* started to rotate and flattened out to a circular disc shaped

like a dinner plate. That is, after all, why the galaxy itself is shaped like a plate.

As the pressure got greater, the temperature got higher, and as the nebula shrank down in size, it speeded up, much like a skater, who goes faster by pulling his or her arms closer in toward the body. Over millions of years, the planets gradually began to be formed from local whirlpools of matter. By this time the temperature at the center of the nebula had reached 10 million degrees, and *thermonuclear reactions* were taking place.

With the sudden outpouring of energy, a violent wind raged through the solar system, stripping away all the gas left over when the nebula contracted. At the center, the sun shone forth and the solar system was born. The sun has been pouring out its energy at about the same

THE MILKY WAY GALAXY

ORBITS OF THE PLANETS

THE EARTH AND MOON

RELATIVE SIZES OF PLANETS AND APPROXIMATE DISTANCES FROM THE SUN

ASTEROID BELT

PLUTO	NEPTUNE	URANUS	SATURN	JUPITER	MARS	EARTH	VENUS	MERCURY
3,675 BILLION MI.	2,797 BILLION MI.	1,787 BILLION MI.	887 MILLION MI.	484 MILLION MI.	141.7 MILLION MI.	93 MILLION MI.	67 MILLION MI.	36 MILLION MI.

MOON

VENUS

MERCURY

SUN SPOTS

EARTH

MARS

SOLAR PROMINENCE

SATURN

JUPITER

URANUS

NEPTUNE

THE SOLAR SYSTEM

AS SEEN LOOKING TOWARD EARTH FROM THE MOON

Stars are born when dense clouds of gas and dust collapse or are compressed by some violent force, such as a nearby exploding star. This region is the Trifid Nebula and is typical of the appearance of young, hot stars.

the tiny planet called Pluto. It is smaller than any of the terrestrial planets and is probably an escaped moon of Neptune. While the four main terrestrial planets are between 3,000 miles and 8,000 miles in diameter, the outer giants are between 30,000 miles and 89,000 miles across.

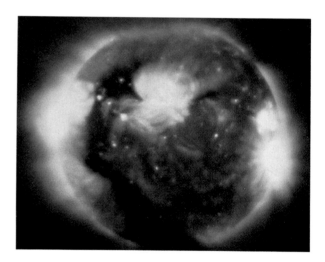

When our sun condensed down into a ball of gas, temperatures rose higher and higher, until nuclear reactions began to radiate energy from the center.

rate ever since, and each second it loses 4 million tons. We receive only a small fraction of this energy, and yet each second the earth is bathed in more energy than man has used since civilization began.

The sun is about 865,000 miles across. At its surface the temperature is a relatively cool 6,000 degrees, compared to about 15 million degrees at the core where the nuclear reactions take place. When the planets formed, they were of two distinct types. Those in the first group, arranged in orbits within about 150 million miles of the sun, are called the *terrestrial planets*. They are hard, rocky bodies like Earth, and they take their name from the Latin word *terra*, for earth. The four terrestrial planets are Mercury, Venus, Earth, and Mars.

Much more dramatic are the outer planets: Jupiter, Saturn, Uranus, and Neptune. They are made up of huge balls of gas and have no solid surface like the terrestrial planets. The outer giants lie between 480 million miles and 4,500 million miles from the sun. Beyond them lies

Opposite page: Jupiter was one of the great planets known to the ancients. In 1609 it was viewed by Galileo, who discovered four moons orbiting the planet.

Robot Explorers

All four terrestrial planets were visible to ancient *astronomers*. Of the outer planets, though, only Jupiter and Saturn could be seen before the invention of the telescope. Unlike stars, planets have no light of their own. They shine in the night sky and look like stars because they reflect light given out by the sun. The moon, too, has no light of its own, but we see it because it reflects the sun's light. Light does not maintain its strength with distance. If it did, we would see the night sky as a great sheet of light from all the stars that exist in space.

Light decreases on what is called the *inverse square law*. If one object is twice as far away as another, it receives only one-quarter the light that reaches the nearest object. If it is five times as far away it receives twenty-five times less light. Jupiter is about five times farther from the sun than the earth and therefore receives only one twenty-fifth the light Earth receives from the sun. Only those planets close enough to the sun to reflect enough light to be seen from Earth are visible to the unaided eye.

Terrestrial planets, such as Venus, have solid surfaces created by rock and iron that cooled down after the solar system formed more than 4,500 million years ago.

Many spacecraft have been developed to explore terrestrial planets. These include probes built to survive intense heat, like this Pioneer that descended to the surface of Venus in 1978.

When Galileo invented the telescope and used it in 1609 to observe marks on Jupiter, he began a new era for astronomy. Four large moons were discovered orbiting Jupiter. Called appropriately the Galilean moons, they are named Io, Europa, Ganymede, and Callisto. Galileo also discovered rings around Saturn. Uranus was first seen by British astronomer William Herschel in 1781 and Neptune was discovered by two astronomers in 1847. Pluto was discovered by American astronomer Clyde Tombaugh in 1930.

By the late 1950s, the United States had put together a program to explore the solar system with unmanned *robots*. Technical developments had been made which would allow machines to go where humans could not. It was the beginning of the third age planetary discoveries. In the early seventeenth century, the age of naked-eye astronomy gave way to the age of telescopes. Now, in the mid-twentieth century, the age of space exploration is underway.

Engineers faced many problems when they began thinking about how to send spacecraft to the planets. To push a small spacecraft beyond earth's gravity required a rocket with a massive

Left: Some spacecraft are designed to go into orbit around the planets. Others are designed to send probes through the atmosphere to the surface. This Pioneer mission involved two spacecraft, one of which (in the foreground) went into orbit around Mars while the second (background) delivered four probes to the surface of Venus.

Below: Before burning up in the atmosphere the four probes sent back information and provided details about the temperatures and atmospheric conditions. No fly-by spacecraft could have achieved these goals.

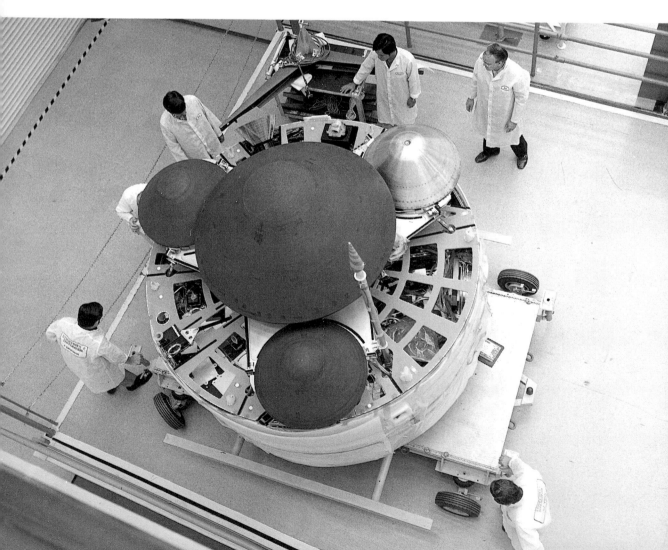

amount of energy. Rockets that large didn't exist, so the first robot explorers were very small and light. To escape earth's grip, a space probe had to be pushed from the surface of the planet to a speed of more than 25,000 MPH. This is called the escape speed, which is about 7,500 MPH more than the speed needed to reach orbit.

One major cause of problems was the fact that scientists did not know exactly where the planets were. They could pinpoint their locations to within a few thousand miles, but that was not accurate enough for a space mission. The probe would have to pioneer its own route by taking measurements as it went. Calculations by controllers on Earth would continue to improve the prediction about the planet's orbit as the spacecraft cruised along toward it. Small mid-course corrections would be made using tiny rocket motors on the spacecraft. This would allow the course, called the *trajectory,* of the

probe to be improved so that it would be as accurate as possible.

NASA engineers realized there were three increasingly complicated levels to planetary exploration. The simplest was a *fly-by* mission, where a spacecraft was put in an orbit of the sun so that it crossed the orbit of the planet it was to explore. The trick was to cross the planet's orbit at the place where the planet would be at that time. Carrying this out required very complex calculations. The nearer planets were the first to be explored as engineers practiced the methods of fly-by. The next level of exploration was to orbit the planet for a full reconnaissance. The most sophisticated type of mission was to land on its surface.

With a fly-by mission, the spacecraft would have only a few hours to gather information as it rushed past the planet. The spacecraft would still be several thousand miles away and would

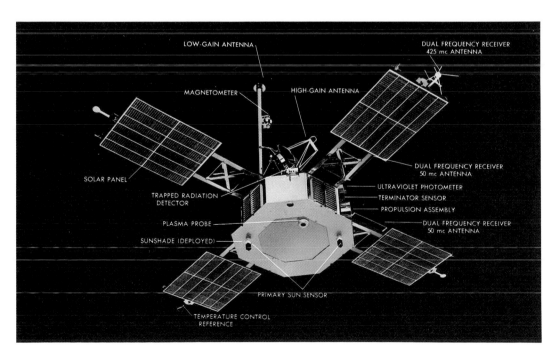

Spacecraft directed toward planets relatively close to the sun use solar panels that gather sunlight and produce electricity. Shown here is *Mariner V* sent to the planet Venus in 1967.

Very large communication antenna are needed to maintain contact with deep space probes. This is the 85-foot antenna at Goldstone in California.

have to keep its instruments facing the surface as it cruised by moving at several thousand miles an hour. To do that, and to keep a radio antenna pointing at earth and solar cells pointing at the sun, they placed the science instruments on a *scan platform*.

The scan platform is a movable hinged structure that sits on the side of the spacecraft. While the spacecraft remains in its fixed attitude, the instruments on the platform can track the planet. This is like panning a camera at a fixed object from a moving train. For the instruments to track the planet properly, careful calculation about the precise position of the planet relative to the spacecraft was required. Not surprisingly, early spacecraft did not have a scan platform. Their instruments remained fixed at one angle to get the best look at the planet as it sped past.

Instruments mounted on a scan platform, which swivels, keep a constant watch on the planet as the spacecraft speeds past it. The scientific instruments continually gather detailed information about atmosphere and about the surface conditions.

For spacecraft destined to fly by Mercury, Venus, or Mars, electrical power was provided by *solar cells*. Farther away from the sun, cells could not produce enough electrical power because the sunlight was too weak. Instead, small nuclear power plants were necessary. Because spacecraft with solar cells had to have one side continually facing the sun, the probe itself had to be kept stable in one fixed attitude. With nuclear power plants, the spacecraft could be spun slowly around its center for stability.

Above all else, NASA needed a powerful net-work of ground stations to transmit and pick up signals to and from the spacecraft. Contact would have to be maintained at all times, and that called for tracking stations all around the globe. As the earth turned on its axis, the signals would shift from one station to the next. Big dish antennas were built at Goldstone in California, Johannesburg in South Africa, and Woomera in Australia.

NASA eventually shut down the station in South Africa and operated a replacement one from outside Madrid in Spain.

To Giant Jupiter

The first probes launched to the planets were part of the Mariner family. Engineers decided that the needs of robot spacecraft were so similar they could design a standard vehicle and modify it for missions to different planets. All Mariners were equipped with small thrusters to maintain a fixed attitude in space. This would keep the solar panels facing the sun for continuous electrical power. In the brief periods when the spacecraft pointed away from the sun to make a mid-course correction, battery power would be used.

The first Mariners were built for a mission to Venus in 1962. Each weighed 447 pounds and had two solar panels. For a mission to Mars in 1964, the Mariner spacecraft weighed 575 pounds and had four solar panels, because the spacecraft would be flying away from the sun and collecting less energy. In attempts to explore Venus and Mars, only one probe to each planet was launched successfully because of failures in the launching rockets. It was for this reason that NASA developed the concept of

Mariner spacecraft built to visit Mercury, Venus, and Mars were provided with systems to keep them operating over periods from one to two years. All had solar cell panels and a main communication antenna to transmit the information they picked up directly to Earth.

Above: Interest focused on Jupiter as a miniature solar system because it was known to have four comparatively large moons.

building two identical spacecraft for each launch opportunity.

Launch opportunities, called *windows,* occur when Earth and another planet are aligned correctly for the minimum amount of rocket power needed to put the probe on its proper course. For Venus, launch windows occur at intervals of about 17 months; for Mars, they occur about every 25 months. NASA used these launch opportunities to send missions to Venus in 1962, 1967, 1973, and 1978. Missions to Mars were launched in 1964, 1969, 1971, and 1975. One spacecraft, *Mariner 10,* launched in 1973, flew past Venus and went on to fly past Mercury, the innermost planet in the solar system.

While NASA was developing this fleet of planetary probes, scientists and engineers began thinking about the next big challenge, the giant outer planets. Mercury and Venus are inside the earth's orbit, which lies 93 million miles out from the sun. Mars, at 141.5 million miles from the sun, lies outside the earth's orbit.

The single most attractive feature of Saturn is its ring system, which can be seen clearly even through a small telescope. Space scientists were eager to explore Saturn because it is so distant and so little has been known about it.

17

Pioneer, a completely different spacecraft from the Mariner vehicles, was built to fly first through the asteroid belt and then on to a close encounter with giant Jupiter.

Jupiter, the nearest of the giant outer planets and the next beyond Mars, lies more than 483 million miles from the sun. Its orbit lies 390 million miles beyond the orbit of Earth.

Between Mars and Jupiter lies the asteroid belt, a broad expanse of rocky debris left over from the formation of the solar system. From telescope observations, astronomers knew it was a hazardous place littered with boulders, rocks, and tiny particles of dust. Nobody knew precisely where the belt started and stopped. General opinion was that the belt began around 180 million miles out from the sun and ended at about 350 million miles. The spacecraft sent to Jupiter and beyond would not only have to survive its journey through the belt, it would also have to travel longer to reach its destination.

Flight times to any of the inner planets are less than one year. It would take a spacecraft nearly two years to reach Jupiter, although launch opportunities came around every thirteen months. By the late 1960s, NASA decided on a dual mission to Jupiter: one spacecraft would be launched in March of 1972 and a second in April of 1973. The spacecraft were of a completely different design than any of the Mariner probes. They were named Pioneer.

Pioneer was built by TRW, an experienced aerospace company based in California. Each spacecraft weighed 570 pounds, about the same as *Mariner 4,* sent on the first fly-by of Mars. But the similarity ended there. Pioneer was *spin-stabilized,* rolling around its center of gravity at no more than four or five revolutions each

Both Pioneers were assembled at the NASA Ames Research Center and delivered to Cape Canaveral, where they were installed in special shrouds before being fixed to the top of the launch rocket.

Atlas-Centaur launched this Pioneer spacecraft toward Jupiter in 1972. It took nearly two years to reach the planet.

minute. This movement was sufficient to keep the spacecraft stable and pointing in a fixed direction.

Pioneer was made to spin for stability because fuel for attitude thrusters like the Mariner used would add weight. The weight of the probe had to be tightly limited for launching. To reach Jupiter within two years, the launching rocket would have to push Pioneer faster than it pushed the Mariners to Venus or Mars. Because Pioneer would travel far from Earth, it had a big 9-foot

diameter dish antenna to receive and transmit signals from ground controllers. Behind the big dish were the spacecraft systems and experiments. To power the systems, four small nuclear power plants were attached in pairs to booms that kept them an appropriate distance away from the experiments.

The systems included batteries, propellant fuel for making course corrections on the way to Jupiter, and a computer to control all the many different functions of the other systems. The ex-

Boosted to an escape speed of more than 25,000 MPH, Pioneer separated from its launch rocket and deployed its scientific instruments plus two booms carrying four radio-isotope generators to produce electrical power.

periments were of two types: those that would monitor conditions on the way and those designed to record details about the giant planet itself. One important job was to record hits on the probe from tiny particles in the asteroid belt and gather information about how dense the dust layers were and what threat they might pose to future probes.

Pioneer 10 was the first probe launched by Atlas Centaur rocket from Cape Canaveral on March 2, 1972. It was placed on such an accurate course that all the way to Jupiter only one minor correction of about 30 MPH was necessary. *Pioneer 10* was accelerated to a speed of just over 32,000 MPH by its launcher. Speeding past the orbit of the moon only 11 hours into its mission, *Pioneer 10* began a flight

that would last more than 22 months before it passed the giant planet Jupiter 80,500 miles above its cloud tops.

Just over four months after launch, *Pioneer 10* entered the asteroid belt and its detectors showed no visible sign of increased dust. Some scientists feared that the spacecraft would be destroyed in the belt, and others thought that it would be severely damaged. As the months rolled by and it flew deeper into the belt, controllers watched anxiously for signs of increased dust. *Pioneer 10* left the far side of the asteroid belt in early February, 1973, eleven months after launch, working well on course for Jupiter.

Pioneer 10 flew past Jupiter on December 3, 1973, having made important measurements of the solar system at a distance three times far-

Left: One target for Pioneer's camera and scientific instruments is this huge red spot in Jupiter's atmosphere, 30,000 miles long and 8,000 miles wide. By comparison, Earth is smaller than the diameter of this unusual spot, which has been seen from Earth for more than 300 years.

Below: Pioneer II flew past Jupiter in early December, 1974, and took this photograph showing the North Pole from a distance of more than 200,000 miles.

ther from the sun than any spacecraft had been before. *Pioneer 10* discovered around Jupiter a huge magnetic field. It was more than 18 million miles across and between 4 and 30 times stronger than Earth's magnetic field. The probe also recorded a giant storm that erupted on the sun and sent radiation past the spacecraft.

Pioneer 11, which was launched on April 5, 1973, followed its predecessor to Jupiter and reached the planet on December 3, 1974. This time the miss distance was only 25,850 miles, because *Pioneer 11* was being targeted to visit another planet after Jupiter. By flying close to Jupiter, *Pioneer 11's* course was deflected by the planet's huge gravity field, 318 times that of earth. This added energy flung the probe around

Jupiter and off on a precise course for the ring-ed planet Saturn.

Pioneer 10 headed for the edge of the solar system and would encounter no more planets. *Pioneer 11,* meanwhile, reached Saturn in late August, 1979, and provided the first close look at this beautiful world and its retinue of moons. *Pioneer 11* passed within 13,300 miles of Saturn and went on to the depths of the solar system. Both Pioneers had done a remarkable job, truly pioneering for the future. The next mission would carry out a full survey of not only Jupiter and Saturn, but of Uranus and Neptune as well.

Called Voyager, the mission built to follow the two Pioneers would take advantage of a unique opportunity. Once in approximately

Pioneer II went on to take a remarkable series of photographs of the beautiful ringed planet Saturn. Compare the quality of this picture with that on page 30, taken by Voyager a few years later.

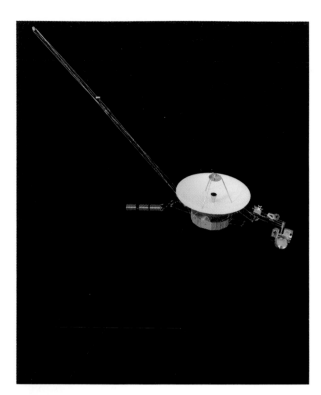

The big Voyager spacecraft began its journey to the outer solar system in 1977. Voyager carried a complex set of scientific instruments and two very powerful television cameras.

years. With the exception of tiny Pluto, all the outer giants would be surveyed within the expected life of a manmade robot. Without the planetary alignment permitting gravity turns to speed the spacecraft at each planet, a trip to distant Uranus would take at least 40 years. It was an opportunity that would not return before the twenty-second century.

The two Voyagers were very different from the Pioneers. They were based on NASA's experience with designing and managing the Mariner spacecraft at the Jet Propulsion Laboratory (JPL). Voyager was not spin-stabilized like Pioneer. It could handle enough weight to carry attitude control thrusters so it would cruise through space in a fixed attitude. The two spacecraft were designed to operate farther into the solar system than any previous probes and carried special heat blankets to keep them warm.

Like Pioneer, the Voyager design was dominated by a large dish antenna; it was 12 feet in diameter. Behind the dish, the main frame of the spacecraft took the form of a ten-sided box 6 feet across and 18 inches deep. Inside were computers to run the probe and its experiments, batteries, propellant tanks for maneuvering thrusters, and many other components. A large boom carried experiments and instruments, including two TV cameras. Three nuclear power plants were fixed to the end of a second boom. A third boom 42 feet long held instruments to measure magnetic fields.

Weighing 1,797 pounds, Voyager was more than three times heavier than Pioneer. To boost it on its way, it carried a 2,758-pound rocket

every 170 years all the outer planets are aligned so that a spacecraft launched from Earth can make a grand tour of the outer solar system. By using the gravity turn at Jupiter, *Pioneer 11* reached Saturn less than 8 years after launch. A direct mission to Saturn, bypassing Jupiter, would have taken three times as long, and the probe would not have survived to make observations.

Voyager would make gravity turns at Jupiter, Saturn, and Uranus to reach Neptune within 12

Opposite page: **Packed up and ready for launch, the Voyager spacecraft is put through tests to ensure that the complex spacecraft will survive its long voyage to Jupiter and the outer planets in the solar system.**

motor. Altogether, the spacecraft totaled 4,555 pounds, eight times the weight of Pioneer. To lift this combination rocket module and spacecraft into space, NASA's biggest launcher was used. The first, *Voyager 2,* was launched by the powerful Titan Centaur rocket on August 20, 1977. *Voyager 1* followed sixteen days later and overtook *Voyager 2* in the asteroid belt.

Like Pioneer before it, Voyager had no problem in the asteroid belt. Both spacecraft emerged safe on the other side and cruised toward their first objective. A notable space first was achieved. On September 18, 1977, *Voyager 1* transmitted a TV picture with the earth and moon in the same image. Detailed views of Jupiter began coming in to the mission control center at JPL in mid-January, 1979. *Voyager 1* was 29 million miles away and closing in on Jupiter.

Jupiter has a large number of satellites. The four Galilean moons, Io, Europa, Ganymede, and Callisto, are the most interesting because they are like small terrestrial planets. Each has

evolved differently in keeping with its position around Jupiter. *Voyager 1* crossed the orbit of the outermost known moon at a distance of 14.3 million miles from the planet. Nearly four weeks later, on March 5, 1979, it reached the point of closest approach, 172,250 miles above Jupiter's clouds.

Voyager made many measurements, probing further the mystery of the planet's interior. Unlike terrestrial planets, which are made up of rock and iron, the four outer planets are giant balls of gas surrounding small cores of rock. Jupiter captured most of the hydrogen gas left over at the formation of the solar system. It is a truly enormous world, 89,000 miles across at the equator, compared to Earth's 7,900-mile

This 43-foot boom has to be supported on Earth because of the pull of gravity. Extended in space, it provided detailed information about Jupiter's magnetic field.

diameter. Jupiter is big enough to contain more than 1,300 planets the size of Earth.

Jupiter spins around once in just under 10 hours, creating broad belts of cloud and gas around the planet. It spins so fast that the planet is actually flattened at the poles. Voyager pro-vided information that helps build a picture of what Jupiter must be like below the swirling and sometimes violent outer atmosphere.

About 13,000 miles below the clouds, the hydrogen that makes up most of the planet's in-terior is compressed from a liquid to a solid

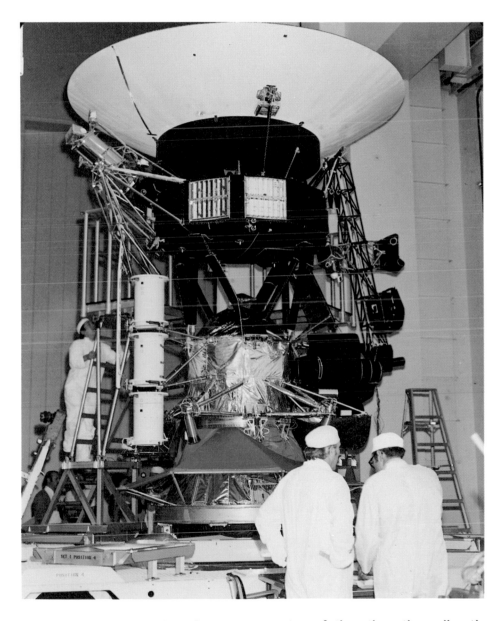

Looking like three small canisters, one on top of the other, the radioactive generators are designed to produce electrical power for Voyager for its long mission through the solar system. Note the large 12-foot diameter communication antenna on top of the spacecraft.

MODEL OF JUPITER INTERIOR

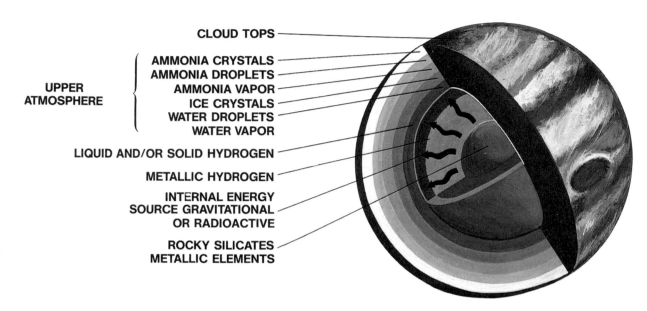

CLOUD TOPS

AMMONIA CRYSTALS
AMMONIA DROPLETS
AMMONIA VAPOR
ICE CRYSTALS
WATER DROPLETS
WATER VAPOR

UPPER ATMOSPHERE

LIQUID AND/OR SOLID HYDROGEN

METALLIC HYDROGEN

INTERNAL ENERGY SOURCE GRAVITATIONAL OR RADIOACTIVE

ROCKY SILICATES METALLIC ELEMENTS

Above: Although the interior of Jupiter has not yet been probed, scientific information gathered from Pioneer and Voyager spacecraft has enabled scientists to make this primitive model to portray what they believe the interior is like.

state. There is no obvious separation where the hydrogen gas turns from liquid to solid. The change from one state to the other occurs in stages, across a depth of several hundred miles at each stage. At a depth of 31,000 miles the solids, called metallic hydrogen, give way to a shallow sea of liquid helium. Farther down lies the surface of a core made from rock and dense metals no more than a few hundred miles across.

Beyond the poisonous clouds of this strange and bizarre world, the Voyager spacecraft discovered wonders never imagined before. The cameras on *Voyager 1* revealed a thin ring of particles only 18 miles thick orbiting the planet 35,400 miles above the clouds. Other pictures showed continuously erupting volcanoes on the moon Io, sending fountains of boiling sulphur more than a hundred miles into the sky. Almost

Seen from the cameras of Voyager as it approached Jupiter, this magnificent view is considerably better than anything returned by the Pioneer spacecraft. Notice the moon Io moving across the visible surface of the planet and the great red spot floating suspended in the planet's southern atmospheric belt.

the size of Earth's moon, Europa was seen to be covered with frozen cracks in the crusted surface of what seemed like a dirty snowball.

Voyager 2 swept through the complex of Jupiter's satellite system in mid-July, 1979. The spacecraft passed within 404,000 miles of the cloud tops to add its own wealth of information about this strange planet and its moons. Both Voyagers were targeted for a close encounter with the planet Saturn more than two years after they left Jupiter. It was to be the start of an exciting journey involving three more giant planets.

Violent winds traveling at nearly 300 MPH create storms and turbulence in the outer atmosphere of Jupiter. This picture was taken from a distance of more than 2 million miles.

The Ringed Planets

Biggest and closest to Earth of all the outer planets, giant Jupiter had been watched closely by astronomers for more than three hundred years. When the four Pioneer and Voyager spacecraft made close observations of it between 1973 and 1979 during their historic fly-by missions, scientists gathered valuable informa-

Voyager 2 shot this view of Saturn and its rings after passing Jupiter and following *Voyager 1* to the ringed planet. Note the atmospheric turbulence towards the pole.

tion that would keep them busy for years. Some scientists, however, were more interested in Saturn, long adored for its beautiful rings seen clearly even through a small telescope.

At a distance of about 887 million miles, Saturn is nearly twice as far away from the sun as Jupiter. Saturn gets 90 times less light from the sun than we get on Earth, and from that distance the sky is always black. To Saturn the sun appears as merely a very bright star. The planet itself is 75,000 miles in diameter, which makes it noticeably smaller than Jupiter. It is believed to have the same layers of hydrogen gas, metallic hydrogen, and rocky core.

The most prominent feature of Saturn, of course, is its splendid ring system. Many ideas were offered as to what these rings could be. It was not long, however, before scientists calculated that the rings had to be made up from millions of tiny pebbles or small rocks. Orbiting the planet in one gigantic convoy, they look like a solid sheet from a distance. In fact, they are laid out in several different ring systems, as Voyager was to show.

Observations from Earth showed that the rings have an inside edge only 4,000 miles above the clouds and extend to a distance of 186,400 miles at the outside edge. The enormous disc is about 372,800 miles across. In other words, the rings of Saturn would more than cover the distance between Earth and the moon, which is about 240,000 miles.

Saturn has several moons, some of which are very interesting. The biggest of these natural satellites — there are at least 18 — is Titan, 3,200 miles in diameter. As a moon, Titan is second only in size to Ganymede, nearly 3,300 miles across, which orbits Jupiter. Viewing Titan by telescope from Earth, astronomers have determined that Titan has an atmosphere. Some scientists feel that it might be a good place for life to develop. To find out if that could be true, they programmed Voyager to make a special scan of the atmosphere.

Like Jupiter, Saturn has many moons, several of which were viewed at reasonably close range by the Voyager cameras. This is not one single picture but a mosaic of several pictures made to show what Saturn might look like from the vicinity of one of its moons.

Above: **Nobody really understood the beautiful and complex ring system of Saturn until the Voyager spacecraft took a series of views to chart the entire area.**

Before the two Voyagers left to go their separate ways, scientists programmed them for the most intensive survey of Saturn likely to be conducted for several years to come.

Of all the discoveries at Saturn, perhaps the strangest concerns the moon Titan. Careful measurements made by both spacecraft reduced the size of the planet about 300 miles compared with calculations based on telescope observations from Earth. Titan has a dense atmosphere, and astronomers had measured the outer edge of the murky mist that envelops the moon, thinking it to be the surface.

Instruments on the Voyagers detected mainly nitrogen in an atmosphere much more dense than that on Earth. Another common gas on Titan is methane. Because of the low

The other moons of Saturn are much smaller. Dione is the next largest at just under 700 miles in diameter. Seven other moons are smaller still, down to a diameter of 137 miles. The rest are just big chunks of rock. Three moons, Mimas, Enceladus, and Tethys, orbit Saturn within the very thin outer rings. When the Voyagers reached Saturn, they discovered gaps within the rings, caused by tiny moonlets shepherding the pebbles by nudging them back and forth, which created a clear space on either side!

The first to arrive was *Voyager 1,* which passed within 78,300 miles of Saturn on November 12, 1980. It was followed by *Voyager 2,* closing to within 62,760 miles on August 26, 1981.

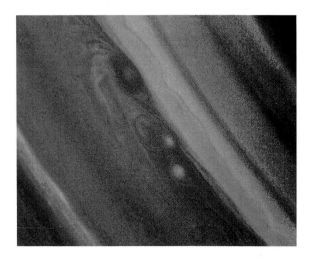

Viewing from a distance of more than 4 million miles on August 19, 1981, *Voyager 2* begins a sequence of pictures to show changes in the atmosphere. From these pictures, scientists will obtain vital clues to the planet's behavior.

Essential for sustaining a major expedition to the moon and the planets, this reusable spaceplane was designed by rocket engineers in the 1950s. The rocket motor that boosted it into orbit is seen falling away.

Plans to explore Mars have existed since the beginning of the space age in the late 1950s. Before that, people thought that the best way to explore the planets would begin with a reusable shuttle followed by a big wheel-shaped space station. Werner von Braun, the man who designed and built the mighty Saturn rockets that took men to the moon, developed such a plan. He saw the space station as a stepping stone to the moon and Mars.

Von Braun was wrong about the way men would first go into space, but he was right about the importance of a space station. NASA is designing a space station to be assembled in earth orbit during the mid-1990s. It will be a suitable place from which to begin the colonization of the moon and Mars. It takes less rocket power to go to the moon from earth orbit than it does to go from the surface of the earth to a space station only 250 miles up.

When Apollo astronauts went to the moon, the chances that they might bring back bugs were very slim. If there *is* life on Mars, it could mean disease and terrible plagues for Earth if

Changes do occur on the surface of Mars, as shown here by a picture taken May 18, 1979, from the *Viking 2* lander touchdown site. The photo reveals water ice on rocks and soil. Robot spacecraft that return to Earth with samples removed from the surface of Mars may be contaminated and will have to be de-contaminated at an earth-orbiting space station.

those microbes mixed with germs in the atmosphere. A space station would be a suitable place for returning astronauts to stay while scientists tested tham and their samples for signs of living organisms. An epidemic of Martian bugs could prove fatal.

Before humans go to Mars, scientists need more information about the planet itself. So far only two landers have sampled the surface at two sites. The next spacecraft to go there will have to extend that survey. First, a very extensive survey from orbit will continue the mapping work begun by *Mariner 9* and the two Viking orbiters. Then sites for a more sophisticated robot lander will be chosen.

The Viking orbiter cameras were able to see objects down to about 260 feet across. Scientists need to improve the equipment so it will photograph much smaller objects. They would also like to be able to measure accurately the

NASA plans to assemble in the mid-1990s a space station with the capability of serving as a receiving base for samples of moon rock. This would help biologists inspect the samples to see if they carry any harmful organisms.

Next in the sequence of robot spacecraft to visit the Red Planet will be the NASA Mars Observer, to be launched in the early 1990s. This spacecraft will map the surface in great detail, preparing the way for the next planned phase in the exploration of Mars.

height of hills, mountains, volcanoes, and valleys. They plan to do this by sending a radio signal to the ground from a spacecraft in a precisely circular orbit and measuring the time it takes to return. In addition scientists will accurately measure the temperature and the wind conditions to understand processes in the atmosphere that affect the movement of dust and sand.

The next expedition to the Red Planet, the NASA Mars Observer mission, will do all these things. To be launched in September, 1992, the 4,700-pound spacecraft will be sent on its way by the shuttle. A year later it will go into orbit around Mars only 224 miles above the surface and continue to operate for more than a full Mar-

tian year, or two years on Earth. It will be the first of a series of spacecraft aimed at preparing the way for manned landings.

Nobody knows exactly what the next step will be. Almost certain to follow Mars Observer, however, is a sample-return flight. In this flight, a Mars rover would roam across the surface and explore different sites. The rover, which might be about 20 feet long and 6 feet wide, would be made up of three cabs linked together like trucks behind a locomotive. The cabs would have two wheels, each more than 3 feet in diameter. These would allow it to climb over rocks and boulders. The cabs would be linked with flexible ties allowing the rover to snake across the rocky surface.

To explore widely different geographic regions on the surface of Mars, a rover will be essential equipment. This artist's impression shows one concept under study by NASA.

The Mars rover would weigh about 1,500 pounds and carry its own guidance and navigation equipment. Controllers on earth could guide it via TV screens, or it could be programmed to pick its own course. The rover would probably roam about 3,000 feet a day and collect samples to carry back to the landing site. After the samples had been put aboard a return vehicle, the rover would go off on its own again to continue its exploration, sending TV pictures back to earth.

NASA scientists can only guess when such a mission might take place. A typical schedule could begin with launch toward Mars in December, 1998. Arriving at the Red Planet in late 1999, the spacecraft would set the rover down on the surface to begin a long survey of the area. The position of the planets at that time would not permit a return flight to Earth before January, 2001. The rover would have more that a year to gather samples. Under this plan, the samples would arrive back at the space station in November, 2001.

Because launch windows to Mars only come around every 25 months, advance planning is particularly important if opportunities are not to be missed. The timing of the launch windows can also affect the length of time between landing on Mars and taking off. For example, if launched in 1996, the return rocket would have to wait only eleven months before it could take off for Earth. If launched at the end of the year 2000, it would have to wait eighteen months.

Some scientists maintain that the best way to reach Mars is to first put a base on the moon. Before that could happen, orbiters would have to map the moon's surface more accurately than Apollo did in its six successful missions between 1969 and 1972. Detailed reconnaissance would be carried out by robot rovers like those planned for Mars. In fact, similar vehicles might be suitable for both worlds. Manned flights might then begin by the year 2000, while detailed surveys using robots were under way at Mars.

Between 2005 and 2010 a construction base could begin, with four landings each year to bring supplies and carry out the work. Manned flights to Mars would be considerably more economical if they could use oxygen taken from rocks on the moon. The lunar base would provide the oxygen-processing plant to help power the rocket ships taking men to Mars. Fueled

This artist's illustration depicts a Mars sample-return mission, with the top stage lifting off to return to Earth.

with hydrogen carried up from Earth, the Mars ships could depart the earth-moon system for planet Mars by 2011.

Scientists would want to set up a base on Mars as they had on the moon, providing two research stations similar to United States stations in Antarctica. They would use them as base camps and travel far across the surface in vehicles developed from the unmanned rover program of the 1990s. Teams of up to four people could travel several days at a time, living in the vehicle and using it to carry rock and soil samples.

Another design for a Mars soil sample-return flight might require the vehicle to touch down in one spot and obtain all its samples without using a rover. A combination of a rover mission and a sample-return flight might rendezvous with separate vehicles at the surface of Mars.

Engineers have proposed this simplified lander-rover developed from the Viking program.

Before men set up the first Mars base, many rovers and sample-return missions may have taken place. This particular vehicle is probing rocks some distance away from the lander.

Back at the main camp, greenhouses would provide most of the food, with compressed carbon dioxide from the Martian atmosphere used to help plants produce oxygen. Living quarters would be modules weighing 38,000 pounds each, similar to the type used in NASA's first space station in the mid-1990s. They would be buried under 3 feet of soil to protect people from the sun's radiation. Although Mars is much farther from the sun than the Earth, its atmosphere has no protective screen as ours does.

Launch and landing sites for rockets coming to and from the base would be made from soilbased concrete. Special maintenance facilities would keep all the machinery working, and small nuclear generators would provide all the electrical power. Because many areas on Mars are thought to have water locked up as ice just below the surface, wells would break down this permafrost and provide running water for drinking and washing. Because Mars has one-third the gravity of Earth, there would be no problem taking a shower.

For really distant surveys, explorers would take to the air, flying great distances in small glider-like planes. Using tiny rocket thrusters to take off and land, these Martian *microlights* would be kept in the air by propellers slowly moving them along at about 50 MPH. Scientists would take to the air to map new areas and search for canyons, craters, and ridges to explore. Eventually, people would transfer between the moon and Mars bases, perhaps collecting together on Mars in the year 2019 to celebrate the 50th anniversary of the first manned landing on the moon.

Opposite page: Within the next twenty years, a Mars base like this one may very well become reality.

Why go to Mars?

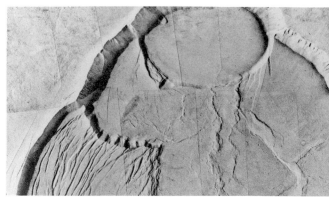

Above: Great wonders await exploration by robots and human explorers in the next twenty or thirty years. This spectacular view of the top of Olympus Mons, the biggest volcano in the solar system, shows it to be more than 90,000 feet high – about three times the height of Mount Everest!

Mars science contains many valuable lessons for the study of Earth, its history, and its resources. Studying the evolution of distant worlds helps us to understand some of the conditions involved in forming the features on the surface of Earth.

Space flight is expensive. To send men to Mars will cost billions of dollars. So why do it? Robots are cheaper and can do almost the same job of surveying and taking pictures. Would it not be better to spend less money on more unmanned spacecraft like Viking, the rover, and the sample-return vehicle NASA will probably develop for the late 1990s? After all, if the mission fails, no lives will be lost.

These are powerful arguments. For thousands of years, human beings had no option. If they wanted to find out about a place, they had to visit it themselves. In the last 50 years, great progress with electronic devices has given us the choice of sending a robot or going in person. The space program itself is an example of the breakthrough in automation and *robotics.* Some people believe it has given humans the chance to do more dangerous jobs without risk, because they can build machines to carry out their work.

Other people say that the human race has a responsibility to explore the worlds around it. They see it as part of progress; without human exploration we would not make great discoveries necessary to improve our quality of life. Better hospitals, new drugs to help sick people, improved means of travel, and more reliable machines can all result from space exploration. The Apollo moon program has shown this to be true.

It is estimated that the economy of the United States received in return seven times what it paid for Apollo. In other words, for each dollar spent on Apollo, the nation got seven dollars back. This money came from improved exports, higher quality electronics, and better products. Those figures do not take into account other benefits, such as an improved understanding of our own world gained from close examination of the moon.

What might we get back from Mars if we send people there? The moon goal, set by President Kennedy in 1961, forced people to develop rockets and spacecraft that would never have built without that challenge. So too would a Mars mission bring enormous benefits for people everywhere. The technology necessary to run a Mars program would provide rockets and spacecraft to mine valuable minerals.

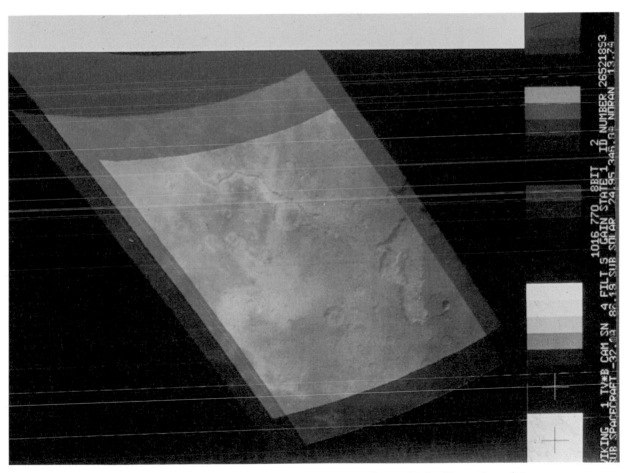

Many detailed and complex techniques were used to obtain the color pictures returned by the Viking orbiter and lander spacecraft. Seen here, different filters overlaid onto a single reproduction provide the color build-up necessary to achieve the correct tone and texture.

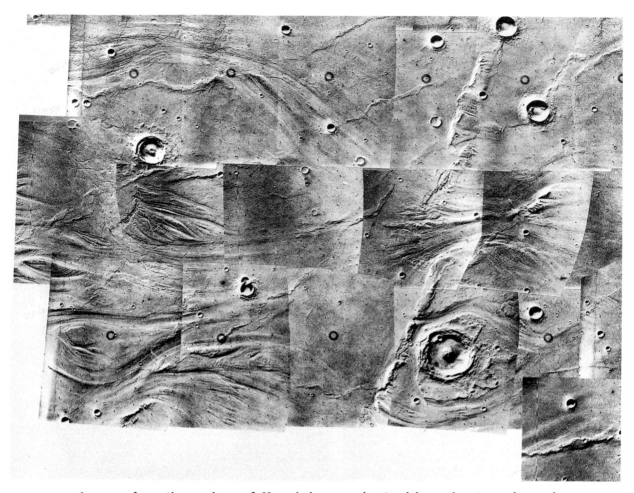

Lessons from the geology of Mars help us understand how planets evolve and change through billions of years. This picture shows detailed evidence of water flows and is similar to sea floor features on Earth.

Earth is running out of important materials that are impossible to produce artificially. These materials are necessary for certain electronic products, such as heart pacemakers and miniature computers. Many of these materials are found on the moon and Mars. With the technology needed to set up a Mars base, we could mine *asteroids,* huge rocks and boulders deep in the solar system containing rare materials. Asteroids could be towed back to the vicinity of Earth and their resources used over many years. Regular trips from the moon and Mars could help replenish diminishing supplies of these minerals on Earth.

Another equally important advantage is harder to measure. By going to the moon, we learned how beautiful our own planet is in the vastness of space. We learned how hostile other worlds are and how precious our own planet is. We also learned how fragile Earth is and how easily the balance of nature can be upset, putting at risk our own lives and those of others. The Apollo program saw the beginning of manned planetary exploration, but it also created concern about the environment and about the delicate balance of nature all over the planet.

By going to Mars, we can improve our understanding of how to care for our earth. Mars seems to be following a sequence not unlike that Earth has been through, although at a much slower pace. There is abundant evidence that water flowed freely on Mars not so long ago and that rivers carved deep gorges between mountains and canyons. We need to understand the processes that caused that to start and then to stop. We may discover important information about the way we are changing the environment of our own planet. If a manned journey to Mars does no more than give us a fresh perspective on our own world, that alone will make it all worthwhile.

Assuming that the present level of effort in the exploration of the solar system is maintained, Mars will probably receive the first human explorers to establish a scientific outpost, similar to those in the Antarctic. These trench marks made by the scoop on the *Viking 1* lander are merely the first in a series of excavations that robot spacecraft will perform between now and the time when human beings set foot on the planet, perhaps as soon as the turn of the century.

GLOSSARY

Aeroshell	A protective shell shaped like a sauce-pan lid, designed to absorb heat built up through friction during entry into the atmosphere of Earth or another planet.
Apollo	The NASA manned spaceflight project of the 1960s and early 1970s devised to land astronauts on the surface of the moon.
Asteroids	Numerous small rocks, boulders, and dust particles that move around the sun between the orbits of Mars and Jupiter.
Astronomer	The scientist who studies astronomy and usually uses telescopes to make observations of objects in space.
Deimos	The smaller of the two moons of Mars and the one farther away from the planet.
Elliptical	Usually a flattened circle or the shape of an orbit similar to the shape of an ellipse.
Equator	The great circle of a planet that divides it into northern and southern hemispheres.
Fly-by	A mission designed to send a spacecraft traveling past another planet so that it can make a reconnaissance or survey of the planet's physical characteristics.
Irrigation	To supply land with water by means of artificial canals, ditches, or pipes to promote the growth of food crops.
Jet Propulsion Laboratory (JPL)	Owned and operated by the California Institute of Technology, JPL operates as the mission control center for most planetary missions and is responsible for project management.
Langley Research Center	The NASA center responsible for having developed the Viking Lander in the early 1970s.
Launch window	The period of time when a spacecraft can be launched, determined by the alignment of planets, for easiest travel of a probe to its destination.
Marsquakes	Disturbances in the planet Mars that create vibrations or rumblings similar to earthquakes on Earth.
Microlite	A hang-glider fitted with a small engine allowing it to take off and land like a small plane.
NASA	National Aeronautics and Space Administration, set up in October, 1958 for the peaceful exploration of space.
Orbit	The curved path, usually almost circular, followed by a planet or satellite in its motion around another body in space.
Orbital period	The time required for a satellite or a planet to make one full orbit.
Organisms	Any living animal or plant, including any bacteria or virus.
Phobos	The larger of the two moons of Mars and the one closer to the planet.

Red Planet	The popular name given to the planet Mars because of its reddish appearance when viewed through a telescope.
Remote Sensing	Measurement and observation of land or the surface of another planet by examining reflected light or other forms of radiation.
Revolution	One complete turn in a circle, or a complete orbit around another body.
Robotics	The science of automated machines programmed to perform mechanical functions in place of a human being.
Solar system	The system containing the sun and the bodies held in its gravitational field including the planets, the asteroids, and comets.

INDEX

Page numbers in *italics* refer to photographs or illustrations.

919.9   Baker, David
Bak
         Journey to the outer
         planets

DATE DUE

Groveton High School Library
38 State St.
Groveton, NH 03582